Rachel and David are frien
both Jewish but Rachel's fa
Orthodox synagogue and David's family
goes to a Reform synagogue.

"Do you have different things in your
home and synagogue?" asks Rachel.

"I'm not sure," says David. "Let's see!"

"In my house," says Rachel, "we have a mezuzah on the doorpost of our front door, our Shabbat candlesticks and our special candlestick for Hanukkah on a shelf, and a picture of Jerusalem on the wall. And my grandfather always wears his kippah."

"We've got those things too," says David, "and a special seder plate for Passover. And my dad wears a kippah – but usually only when he says prayers."

"Every year, just before Passover, we have to clean our house from top to bottom to make sure that there's no leaven or yeast anywhere – so no biscuit crumbs or bread crumbs, nothing!"

"Same at our house," says David. "Then we have a special meal to remember how God, through Moses, led the Hebrew slaves out of Egypt to freedom. The bitter herbs remind us how hard it was being slaves and the salt water is like the sweat and tears of the Hebrews."

"Yes, and we have sweet wine to celebrate freedom," interrupted Rachel.

"Every Friday, we remember how God created the world and then rested. Just before sunset, I help my mum light two candles to welcome Shabbat into our home," explained Rachel. "She says a blessing in Hebrew. In English, it means:

Blessed are you, O Lord Our God, who commands us to light the Sabbath lights."

"Yes," added David, "and my dad thanks God for the fruit of the vine and we all have a sip of sweet wine. Then he says a blessing over the plaited loaf called a challah and we all eat some."

"Don't you love Shabbat," asked David, "doing no work and being at home with all your family?"

Rachel described what happens when her family goes to the synagogue on Saturday morning.

"My grandfather and brother wear their kippahs and we all walk to synagogue. It is a really big building with a Star of David in the stained-glass window. Our rabbi, Rabbi Daniel, welcomes us and I go upstairs with my mum. My grandfather and brother put on their prayer shawls and sit downstairs."

To Rachel's surprise, David told her that his mum and dad sit together and that his rabbi, Rabbi Sarah, is a woman.

So, some things are the same, some are different.

The most important part of a synagogue is the Ark, a large cupboard. Inside it are kept the Torah scrolls. The Torah is the holy book for Jews.

The scrolls are handwritten in Hebrew. The Rabbi uses a pointer in the shape of a hand to point to the Hebrew letters as he reads.

When the reading is finished, the scrolls are covered in a beautiful velvet cover and bells are put on top of the wooden rollers.

Both Rachel and David agree that it's exciting when the Torah scrolls are taken out of the Ark and processed around the synagogue. Some men touch the scrolls with the fringes of their prayer shawls – "It's to show how special the Torah is," says Rachel.

Neither Rachel nor David can understand Hebrew but they like to hear the stories of Abraham, Moses and Joseph and his brothers when they are told in English.

13

At home, on Saturday evening, it is time to say goodbye to Shabbat until next week. This is called havdalah.

Rachel usually holds the plaited candle; in his family, David usually passes round the spice box for everyone to smell and remember the sweetness of Shabbat.

Then, both Rachel and David, in their different families, are allowed to taste just a drop of sweet Shabbat wine.

"Shavuah tov!" they wish each other –
A happy week!

Shavuah tov!

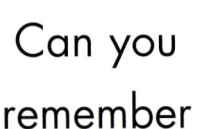

Can you
remember
some of the special

objects and places in
the children's homes

and synagogue?

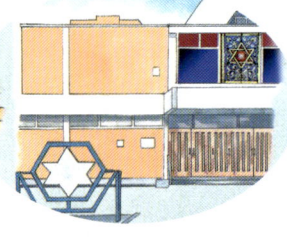

Published by RMEP (Religious and Moral Education Press)
An imprint of Hymns Ancient and Modern Ltd (a registered charity)
St Mary's Works, St Mary's Plain, Norwich, Norfolk NR3 3BH

Copyright © Lynne Broadbent and John Logan 2009

Lynne Broadbent and John Logan have asserted their right under the Copyright,
Designs and Patents Act, 1988, to be identified as Authors of this Work.

First published 2009

ISBN 978-1-85175-379-6

Designed and typeset by Topics – The Creative Partnership, Exeter
Printed in Great Britain by Halstan & Co. Ltd, Amersham, Bucks